# WOODCUTS


David J. Rodman

ISBN 978-0-6151-5876-1


Published by Soluna Hawaii
PO BOX 4476, Kailua-Kona HI 96745
www.solunahawaii.com

*For Judy*

Acknowledgements

To my beloved wife Judy, with whom I have shared more than a third of my life, thank you for being sounding board, cheer leader, editor, critic, and never-hesitating companion as the adventure continues.

To the regular sweat hogs Ngaire, Calley, Rama, Willis and the irregular sweat hogs too, thank you for your prayers and your questions and for persistently asking for a wood-cutting story every Sunday.

To LaDonna Brave Bull Allard, Miles Allard, Felix Kidder: thank you for teaching me, challenging me, and befriending me.

To all of my Sun Dance brothers and sisters, there aren't any words, we'll just keep on dancing together.

# CONTENTS

# Introduction

"A man's reach should exceed his grasp" -- that's an invitation to strive beyond the known limits of our lives, not being stopped by the "knowledge" of what is possible. Something happens when we open up to the world that lies beyond what we directly control and understand. A relationship with that world brings forth possibilities that simply do not exist in the bright clear light of the known. How many great achievements in science, music, mathematics, medicine, art, literature have arisen out of moments of inspiration, or dreams, or other mysterious sources? These flashes seem to illuminate a consciousness ready for them. It's a dance of the ego and the unknown, of seeking and accepting, intention and serendipity.

Software design involves both the clear, planned, controlled logic of computers and also the mysterious, fortunate, even flukish happenstance that leavens any creative endeavor. More than once while working on a difficult project or inventing a software tool, I've had the experience of stumbling away from the terminal in exhaustion, unable to focus any longer, stuck on a particular puzzle, and then returning to the workbench the next day only to find that I'd discovered the answer in the interim, without giving it a moment's conscious thought. Much to my surprise I found I was able to work much more effectively when I gave up the idea that I had to wrestle every problem to a solution in one continuous effort of will. A semblance of balance began to arise between the periods of sustained focus and the periods of living my life away from the computer. And even more surprisingly, the time away from the computer seemed to produce the really inspired ideas, ones that bubbled up unbidden from an unknown, uncontrolled source.

When these gifts were arriving on my threshold I gave no thought to their source – to my mind it was I, of course, and I proceeded to implement them and reap the benefits with the passion of creative youth. No doubt I would have been powerless to exploit these ideas had I not put in so much time learning the tools and techniques of the profession. And had I not been inspired as a child by the magical, mysterious, romantic and fabulously logical universe of what was then a new human endeavor not yet called "Computer Science", I would certainly not have invested all that time in learning the tools and techniques. So, you see? It's a dance. What called to me? And what answered from within me? It was not a plan, goal, or concept. Joseph Campbell would have called it my bliss, and following it the only living possibility. In following your bliss, or in living your vision as the Lakota people say, you are constantly approaching the essence of the dream, vision, inspiration that drew you in the first place and the corresponding essence that has always been within you.

Finding one's vision, making the choice to pursue it, balancing the inner voices that vote on that one way or the other – these things require some kind of spiritual practice; that is, they require some regular focus on the strengthening of the inner spark of life within us. I do not advocate a religion, and I am not saying anything about God. I'm talking about the regular practice of seeking and furthering the core strength that we call spirit. What that is, how it's related to the idea of God, what's happened to the vocabulary of spirituality – all these are subjects for a different time. This book is simply a relaying of some of the gifts I've received while walking the path my spirit has chosen.

The spiritual practice I follow involves cutting firewood once a week and heating up stones in a fire. Once a year I join my good friends and adopted family and participate in the Sun Dance – not the film festival, the ancient ritual. If you don't already know about these ceremonies you're going to learn only a few tidbits here; my purpose is not to explain the ceremonies but to share what goes on within and around me as I participate in them.

Every Saturday I go out onto the rugged and beautiful Hawaiian land near my home, land that was a barren black lava flow not many years ago. Vegetation is sparse and hardy and I can't help but respect the persistence of life as I admire these grasses and trees that have struggled and flourished up out of the raw stone. I am grateful for the life of these kiawe trees, no longer living – some devastated by wildfires or dried up in drought, some having died from an unlucky location – and I am grateful for my part in reaping their energy and bringing them into another place where they help us do our ceremony as they release their substance into the air, into the fire. Walking across the lava carrying a heavy load of wood requires balance and strength and I am grateful for my body, for the purpose that carries me forward, and for the beauty of the place that surrounds and supports me. The vast deep blue of the ocean sprinkled with whitecaps, the parallel blue of the sky sprinkled with clouds, the earthy almost peaty smell of the land, the rolling fields of beige drying fountain grass melting into soft green voluptuous hills sprinkled with sheep, sounds of cars and trucks, birds and goats and my chainsaw, the unyielding hardness of flowing rock beneath my feet. Every week as I cut and gather the wood and dried grass for the fire, I open myself to the land, sky, and sea and contemplate my life and my part in its endless cycles. Over the years I've been doing this weekly chore, how my circumstances have changed, how the conversations I've had with myself while doing this have changed. I think about the people who are coming to the ceremony this week, and the journey each of us has taken to arrive in this circle together.

I toy with the idea of parallels between my experience in cutting the wood and the way the ceremony itself will turn out. And later as we sit in the circle together, I will tell the story of the cutting of the wood, I will share the lessons or questions, the symbols or synchronicities that have populated my consciousness while walking this path. The ceremony, the land, the wood, the ideas and feelings and experiences that surround them – these are great gifts, given to me so that I will share them. What's important is not who gives these gifts, but who receives them.


Mitakuye Oyasin
David J. Rodman, Hawaii, 2006

## Opening Prayer

Right away I'm hearing you say "Prayer? Hang on ... I thought you said you weren't talking about God." Let's just tackle this at the outset. I suppose the most immediate question is "to whom are you praying?" I don't really ask that question – it's become more and more clear to me that the prayer itself is what matters, not the intended recipient. However, I certainly have given a lot of thought to this practice of prayer and how it could possibly make sense, and I'll share some of that with you.

Soon after my 41$^{st}$ birthday I was playing racquetball and suddenly found myself incredibly exhausted after only a short time. Seeking medical help I found out I was suffering from arrhythmia - my heart was beating irregularly, sapping my energy, making it impossible for me to work. The preliminary diagnosis was terrifying – a phenomenon called "IHSS", from which people can simply drop dead without any warning. During a period of about 3 months I underwent various efforts to explain and counteract this affliction. I'm a believer in self-responsibility, I considered myself to be in control of my fate and accountable for my situation whatever it might be, and I was casting about rather desperately for some understanding, some indication of what I could do or had done or ought to do differently. Until then my attitude had been fairly consistent – I'm an entrepreneur, an inventor, I do what I choose to do, I create the results I plan. Here was a very attention-getting example of something that was affecting my life powerfully and directly, yet I had no control over it and no understanding of its operation. As I attempted to find some meaning to it, some lesson to be learned or wisdom to be gained, I started to have the idea that perhaps all of my parts were not lined up in the same direction. "How", I kept asking myself, "am I living out of rhythm with my heart?"

Some years previously I had encountered the sweatlodge and really loved it. I didn't give any thought to the ceremony, the spiritual aspects of the practice, or anything like that. I just really liked how it felt to be huddled there in the dark with those red-hot stones, chanting unknown words in an unknown language, feeling the earth under me and the steam all around me. I was like those folks I often wrote software for, with the attitude "I don't care how it works, I just want the result".

While I was having this bout with arrhythmia a friend who knew of my interest asked if I would help him build a sweatlodge. I had an intuitive sense that this would be good for my heart. It gets good and hot in there and your heart speeds up. I thought perhaps it would speed up to the point where it was beating faster than the irregularity, and straighten itself out, and just stay regular when it slowed down. So I did help him, and we did a ceremony together and while singing the songs in the first round I was very focused on my heart and on hearing its true rhythm, and had an intense attitude of seeking, asking, hoping for a particular healing result. Although I had that vague theory of what might happen I certainly had no idea *how* it might happen and was not particularly interested in that detail. I was in a rudimentary way turning over my fate to an unknown power and sincerely asking for a healing within me.

Now you should know that I considered myself an atheist – in fact, I still do although no one who knows me seems to agree. I learned that word "atheist" when I was 5 years old and it sounded just right –

someone who does not believe in an external all-powerful controlling being who's everywhere and knows everything. Yup, that's me, where do I sign?

So there I was praying, not thinking of myself as praying, and my heart did indeed straighten itself out. Now the first time I was in arrhythmia I was taken to the Cardiac Intensive Care Unit and kept overnight. They cardioverted me, which means they used electric shocks to stop my heartbeat completely and then hoped that it would start back up in normal rhythm. Well, that worked too – after the second try – but gee, which would you rather do?

For a year or so after that I read everything I could get my hands on that had anything to do with the sweatlodge, and also doing what ceremony I was able, which wasn't very much but it included the very basic elements. In one of the books I read there was a brief mention of a Lakota medicine man named Chipps, a close friend of Crazy Horse and the one who taught him how to ride into battle without being injured, based on the interpretation of a vision. They built a sweatlodge together and purified and prayed together.

Crazy Horse was a powerful leader, a hero to his people. The shape of his life was predicted and deeply influenced by the vision he experienced as a young boy. By all accounts he was willful, headstrong, yet he followed a direction he had not intentionally or consciously set. It seemed he had found a balance between his own private choices and the overarching theme of his life; a balance I had begun to long for.

Soon after completing that book, as I pondered more and more deeply the concordance of events that had brought me to this inipi ceremony, it occurred to me that perhaps I ought to pray about my questions and confusions.  My attitude towards prayer at that time was that I was simply calling forth my own inner compass, appealing to my subconscious.  I pushed it a bit this time; I said "Listen, I want to know what a spiritual path is, and am I supposed to be on one?  If there's something I'm supposed to be getting, I'm telling you right now you'd better make it absolutely undeniably crystal clear, because otherwise I'm going to deny it.  It's neon sign or nothing."

Well – four days later I got a call out of nowhere from a man I'd never met.  "Hello, you don't know me, but I'm here with my friend Charles Chipps, and he knows you're a lodge builder.  He is here on the island doing ceremonies and perhaps he'd like to use your lodge."  Charles Chipps, we soon found out, is the great-great-grandson of the man in the book I'd just read.  He spent two weeks with Judy and me, doing ceremonies every day and teaching us.  During that time I set myself two tasks: suspend judgment for the time being so that I can learn as much as possible; and write everything down so I could refer back to it later when my rational mind has a chance to weigh in.  It took me a while to see this: you don't need to cling to rationality, it's not going to go away.  Just because I cannot explain something doesn't mean it cannot be explained, and in any case I will not deny my own experience just because it makes no sense.

I could tell you amazing stories of the events that occurred during those weeks and the ensuing years, and perhaps in another conversation I'll do just that.  But I don't want to distract you from the real invitation represented by this book: find your own mystery, your personal adventure.  Pursue it with integrity and intensity, and follow where it leads you like a dancer.

## Four Trips

After cutting enough wood for tomorrow's ceremony, I set myself the goal of getting it all up to the truck in 4 trips. I cut it into about 10-foot pieces and carried them up next to the truck, then bucked it up from there. As I'm lugging the second trip I realize I'm not going to be able to carry it all in four trips, and anyway I'm running out of light.

I refocus and remember that this whole thing is quite simple – the purpose for cutting the wood is to make the fire, the purpose for the fire is to heat the stones. Everything else is an overlay – not necessarily good or bad, right or wrong, it's all part of the process. As I consider this, fear and shame rise up in me – obviously unrelated to the immediate task, old stuff – and again I refocus and am reminded of the meditation instructions that say when you find your thoughts drifting or, more accurately, arising, just notice that: there is a thought, here is a breath, thinking, breathing, carrying wood, grunting ... fear and shame? Well, it goes back to my struggle to find a balance between ego and mystery. See, I declared that I was going to get all that wood up to the truck in 4 trips. Now I'm renegotiating – reneging on my word, failing to demonstrate integrity, making excuses, bargaining, wanting to strike a deal with the Great Mystery. All right – so, ego says "I WILL accomplish this. I am a man of my word, I have integrity. When I declare a result, I do what it takes to have it happen." The voice of the mystery says "There are things operating that affect you, affect your results, and that you do not cause or control." The voice of self-condemnation says "That's a load of crap – either you keep your word or you don't. Either you measure up or you don't. Either you are worthy or you're not".

So what's the deal? It's a dance. You present your intention, declare your intended outcome. You take action towards having that happen. And you stay conscious – stay aware of the other factors and forces that are present besides your own will power. Recognize what you can affect and what you cannot, and keep on going. So the focus on cause-and-effect gets fuzzier, while the recognition of the mystery emerges. Questions arise that may be relevant and may not be – for example, "Why did I choose this particular goal? Why did I set an intention that I cannot accomplish? Is there another way to achieve the result?" Instead of being blanket condemnations, these questions may illuminate one specific instance while being of no value in another. To open up to the dance is to relinquish ironclad control over the outcome – which is illusory anyway. To open up to the dance is to acknowledge what's so – we accomplish results when there is a concordance of intention, action, and fortune.

And here's a bonus – the opening to the dance is a two-way street. When I'm willing to accept a degree of mystery, I may discover that the mystery is willing to accept a degree of me. To allow myself to remain conscious in the face of an unfolding mysterious concordance of events is also to allow myself to participate in that unfolding without fear of annihilation. It is that fear that prevents the purely ego-based consciousness from dancing and, sadly, from experiencing the vastly expanded possibilities beyond what I myself alone can cause.

Later that week I went back for more wood, trying to get a little ahead. Sometimes it rains on Saturday and then I have to get out at first light to cut the wood Sunday morning. Well, "have to" isn't exactly accurate – it's so beautiful and especially mysterious at dawn out on the land. But anyway, I went back and was thinking about that fear and shame. Fear and shame are words I use to describe a physical sensation. This time I thought "what if I were to feel this during the Sun Dance, what would I do?" Easy question - keep dancing and praying, obviously. So I tried that and how interesting! That feeling shifts to something quite different when I move my inner focus from my head to my gut. I remembered something from Reiki training – close the first chakra and hold that energy in. OK, that probably sounds pretty weird if you're not familiar with the body's energy centers, but I'm telling you this is not hypothetical and can easily be detected and demonstrated scientifically if that matters to you – our bodies do indeed generate energy and there are many foci where that energy is stronger than elsewhere. That's all I'm talking about. Try it. Don't worry about what it means or what you're supposed to believe, just imagine an energy center midway between your anus and genitals, and imagine closing it so that no energy can enter or escape. Try walking around for a while with that in mind, see if you notice anything. For me, on that day, carrying that load of wood, it was an experience of great power and strength. The heated sensation I have identified as fear, shame, guilt, anxiety (subtle variations on the same theme, differing mostly in the mental content that accompanies the sensation) was transformed, at least for that span of time, into simply heat; energy without judgment.

And I wonder now as I'm writing this, is there a connection to the heat of the stones in the lodge? We certainly know that the experience of being in the lodge is very different from one person to the next, sitting next to each other in the same ceremony. And it's also very different for the same person from one week to the next, sitting in the same lodge with the same stones at the same temperature doing the same ceremony. What accounts for the differing responses and inner experiences of this heat? Why is it sometimes just so difficult to feel it neutrally? Why is it healing and strengthening one week and piercing the next? Well, I don't know. Seems to me there's a relationship there, a mind-body-spirit dance, and of course that is exactly what this whole practice is for me – beginning when I go out for the wood.

## That Tree

When I went for wood yesterday I took another look at a tree I've had my eye on for some time. It's a really good tree about 30' tall and with enough branches that it would provide the wood for one ceremony all by itself, with a variety of sizes. But the thing is, it's about 50 feet down a pretty steep incline. It'll be easy enough to fell, but getting it up that hill is going to be rough. So I've been keeping my eye on it and waiting until it seemed like my strength and the weather conditions and everything else were in alignment, just waiting for my relationship with this tree to come into its time.

So yesterday was the day. It was overcast and a little windy, which makes a huge difference compared to the usual blazing sun. I was feeling very strong, my legs good and solid. Funny thing though – my left knee was bothering me just a little. I've had trouble with this knee before, years ago – it kind of "popped" out of place and swelled up. The MDs wanted to do surgery but I did a sweatlodge instead and was truly amazed at the results – I limped into the lodge that day and danced out. Now it's a funny thing this knee is bugging me today because my friend Rich just injured his left knee earlier this week, and I told him I'd pray about it and work on it this week in the lodge. I've had this experience before – the knee is a little stiff and I just carefully but with determination carry on. The thought occurs to me that maybe I'm taking on the injury for my friend, maybe if mine heals his will too. Anyway I do what I do, keep going with respect and attention to the knee and after a while it's just perfect.

I made my way down the slope and felled the tree, cut it into 10-foot lengths and started working them up the hill. As I got the first piece up to the staging area I'd picked out, a raucous cheer rose up just down the coast from me. I thought "Cool! I have a cheering section!" It was the day of the Ironman Triathlon, and the timing was just right - the bikes were going by a few at a time and as they did, there were supporters with their coolers and water bottles yelling and encouraging them. Hee hee! It was great – all the time I'm humping these massive logs up the hill, I've got 20 screaming fans just going nuts: "WOO HOO! GO! GO! GO!"

I got all the wood up to the plateau I was using for staging. This time I didn't seem to want to make a deal about how many trips I'd take to the truck – still feeling very strong, I just carried all that wood, taking my time, resting and drinking water as needed. Then I bucked it all up and loaded it. While I was finishing up, the Ironman supporters were breaking up their little camp, walking back up to their cars and trucks parked down the hill from me. A couple of cars stopped right near me – reorganizing their stuff, it looked like. As they looked at me wielding my chainsaw and loading all this wood into my truck, I looked at them wielding their SPF 50 and reloading all that beer or soda and cold cuts. I was really grateful to them, smiled and waved. I tried to imagine what it was like for them, this guy in long sleeves, thick pants, heavy boots sweating away over this load of wood, smiling and waving. Why's he waving at us? They can't know why I'm thanking them, but they seem to decide "what the heck, it's Hawaii" and wave back. Can they guess how important this must be to me, to work this hard in the noonday Hawaiian sun on a Saturday? It's a thought that comes frequently in similar forms – just a recognition of how much effort I'm willing to invest in this practice – how much doing there is in this form of being.

As I wondered about how the ceremony would be, I just thought "Keep going, take your time, accept the support that comes your way. No limits, no bargains. Relationships arise in their own time, and the dance continues – push enough to be present.

Today lighting the fire I said my prayers, asked for the *peta owihankesni* (eternal fire) to come up in a good way for the sake of all of us coming to pray. I had all the dry grass and tinder and rocks and big logs all arranged as usual, lit the fire from the northeast where the wind was blowing from ... but you know, my mind kind of wandered and more than that, my presence kind of wandered while I was lighting it. I just, I don't know, stopped praying and started thinking about something else. What do you know, the match just barely touched that dry grass and went out. That one piece of grass fizzled and smoked a little and was quiet again. Seems that although it doesn't mater what you're thinking while you're praying, and it doesn't matter what you're doing while you're praying, it sure matters whether you're praying while you're praying. So it took two matches today. The second one, I did exactly the same thing, lit it and touched it to the grass and whoosh.

Woodcuts

# Relativity

"All my relations" is the way it's usually translated. To me, this conveys nothing at all – it sounds like the name of a soap opera. In the Lakota language it's "mitakuye oyas'in". I hear people abbreviate it "mi tak oh ya si", or even "mitak". My friend Lionel always says it slowly and clearly – "mi taku ye o yas' in". I appreciate that – it reminds me to pay attention to the meaning of that phrase, which moves and changes and seems to grow with attention.

"Miye" means "me" or "my". "Taku" means "part of" or "what is". "Oyas'in" means "everything", and carries some of the flavor of "oyate", which means "people" in the sense of "nation" or, broadly, "family" – we speak of the elk nation, the eagle nation. Now, having said what these words mean, I have not told the truth. These words are surely symbols in the Jungian sense – that is, they point to something which is ultimately irrepresentable.

When I say "mitakuye", I am speaking of my relatives, my family, those beings of which I am a part or which are part of me. And isn't that a lovely construct? The "taku" is plugged right into the middle of the "miye" – so the word itself conveys that idea of "central to" or "part of" me. And the plural is the same "mitakuye" also means "our relatives", "part of us", "related to us".

This particular way of expressing the relationships that bind and include us is characteristic of the Lakota language, and that language is an expression of the consciousness of the Lakota people. The choice of what to have abstractions for is deeply influential in the development and flowering of the children who learn to speak that language. You've probably heard the myth that there are 40 words for "snow" in the Inuit language, and as many words for "wave" in Hawaiian. I think there are 17 words for "rain" in the Seattle language, and 22 for "coffee", but I'm not sure. The idea, if not the myth, is sound – it's much more difficult to think about something if you don't have a word for it, and if it's something that has a direct impact on your well being, you probably have concepts for several gradations of it. Hawaiian navigators accomplish miraculous feats by reading the waves and detecting signs of land that are completely invisible to someone without the ability to differentiate those little wavelets. And there are words in Hawaiian for different kinds of waves and different parts of the waves. Computer languages are like this too – the first choice an accomplished programmer will make is what language to use in order best to express the meaning of a program. The Lakota language has lots of words for relationships. There's a separate word for a male's older brother, male's younger brother, female's older brother, female's younger brother, 4 more for sisters. Some words differentiate the speaker's gender. "Do it this way" is different spoken by a man or woman.

Having a specific word for a particular aspect of something certainly makes it more likely that one will perceive that aspect, don't you agree? And having an experience that relates to the word makes it easier to learn and use the word. This has been occurring within me with regard to spirituality. Words that meant less than nothing to me several years ago actually have referents in my experience now, and I think that this is allowing me to be open to learning more about the mysterious and wonderful ways in which all of us affect each other and are related to each other. I would go so far as to say that if you have no

Woodcuts

concept for something, then when it happens to you, you are very unlikely to be conscious of it. I mean, if you don't have a word for "little wave that crosses over big wave in the direction of a land mass", then all you really see is a sort of chaotic interaction of lots of waves. An expansion of perception accompanies an expansion of conception, and it's not at all clear to me which is chicken and which is egg. Either way, I see that now when I participate in a synchronistic event I have a concept for that, mitakuye oyas'in, and so I am able to remain conscious in the midst of this mystery that otherwise might not even be available to me at all.

The legends and myths, the ceremonies and songs that have survived the centuries are captured in an ancient language, an ancient way of expression that is not the same as the way modern Lakota folks chat with each other. When you start to ask about the meaning of the old stories, or of the ceremonies we do each week, the songs, well then you're getting into the mystery. The songs are in the language of metaphor, symbol, image. When I say "mitakuye oyas'in", I am also saying that meaning itself is related to "me" – to the one seeking meaning.

As I went for the wood one Saturday morning a few weeks ago, I was not particularly rushed or even particularly purposeful. It was one of those times when I was just flowing along, open to what might arise. I didn't go to my usual spot but stopped a mile or so away, parked and started walking towards a promising clump of old grey kiawe trees, sun bleached and ready for the fire. I said to myself "I will take two of those trees". As I approached them I saw a good-sized pair of trunks that had fallen years before and were nearly covered by the drying underbrush.

What a strange question struck me just then: would it be wrong to take these fallen trees instead of the ones I had already promised to take? Would I be breaking my word? Was there some reason why those other ones farther down the hill had caught my attention, would I be missing something by forgetting about them? I laughed and remembered what one of my first teachers said to me when I was struggling to get exactly the right configuration of wood for the fire. "The purpose of this fire is to heat the stones." Oh yeah. I'm here to get enough wood to build a fire to heat the stones.

But you know, that series of questions arises out of my attempt to be open to the mystery, to be influenced by or a participant in the great dance of unfolding intertwining events. I'm trying to find my own balance in that dance, to carry forward with my personal intentions and commitments and at the same time to be respectful of the other forces besides my own will that have impact on how events transpire.

I cleared the brush from those fallen trees and cut them into pieces I could carry. Then I continued down the hill to the grove I'd originally chosen and was delighted to discover a much larger cache of good wood than I'd expected. As I cut it I pondered again the meaning of "mitakuye oyas'in" – we are all related. Everything's relative? I wondered – is this any part of what Einstein was talking about? In trying to understand what I'm supposed to do, what my function is – ultimately I guess I'm asking what the meaning of my life is – what's missing is an absolute frame of reference within which I can compare where I am to where I ought to be. OK, I grant you, this is a weird thing to be thinking about while using a chain saw on a tree branch, but there it is. I was cutting away and considering – what gives me the right to cut this wood and take it away? If someone came along and challenged me on this, what would I say? Hmm. Well, I'd say that this wood has more value now that I've cut it than it did before, and by adding that value to it I've acquired the right to enjoy that value. I guess before that I'd have to say that this wood is on public land and I pay my taxes. But someone could easily argue that the wood was very beautiful, that the grey branches against the yellow grass before the blue sea comprised a vista of aesthetic value that I have now destroyed. It could turn into an interesting debate, I'm sure – but my point is, it's not so easy to pin down exactly what standard of value is appropriate here.

By the same token, if I really want to take my place in the great swirl of events, how do I decide where my personal will should give way to that of someone else, or to the non-will of nature unfolding? How do I tell whether my impulse to go in a certain direction is an expression of the natural unfolding of life, or of my ego, or both? I mean, there is not necessarily any conflict between the two. I'm a naturally unfolding life form, am I not?

There's no Archimedean point upon which I can stand outside the realm of conscious desires and judge their relation to the greater container of life that includes consciousness. This is what Einstein realized about matter – there's no absolute fixed frame of reference against which we can measure velocity. "What would the world look like if I were riding on a beam of light?" – what a fabulous question.

Well, yesterday I went back to that same spot. As I parked my truck, I noticed a white van pulling up behind me. I thought "I guess this person thinks I've broken down or gotten a flat and is stopping to help me. How nice!" I got out, prepared to thank this Samaritan and send him on his way, when the other driver got out of his van and asked me in Japanese how to get to Ocean View. He had a sketchy but reasonably accurate map on which someone had marked his destination. Eigo-wo hanashimasu ka? Do you speak English? Nope. Oh boy. I pulled out pretty much my entire Japanese vocabulary and managed to rearrange the words into sentences that I think said "You are here now. You are going there." I pointed him in the right direction and showed him the highway itself and its representation on the map, so he could get his bearings. "That (pointing to the highway) is this (pointing to the line on the map)." Then it occurred to me that I could also help him by telling him about how far it was, so he'd have some idea of when to look for the road signs. I think I said "about an hour and a half" – "ichi ji han gurai" – because I have no idea how to say it in miles and anyway the time is more useful, I think. He thanked me and shook my hand with a grin, and I thanked him too, quite sincerely, because it was really so gratifying. "Wakarismasu ka?" I asked him – "do you understand?". Oh yes, he said, thanks very much!

As I strolled down the hill chuckling, I realized how uplifting that experience had been. Here's someone from another island, thousands of miles away, in a foreign land, does not speak the language. How bravely he has ventured forth to find Ocean View on a Saturday afternoon, with only a sketchy map and no interpreter. How much I enjoyed our opening up this little doorway between his world and mine, sharing a grin and a part of his adventure. I felt a sense of connection, usefulness, efficacy. What a nice gift – turns out this stranger did stop to lend me a hand after all. And when I looked at those trees again, only then did I remember my previous rumination about relativity, about mitakuye oyas'in, about the questions of frame of reference – who's helping whom? Who's getting direction from whom? And it struck me that when I'm willing to open up my path beyond where my ego knows how to go, when I'm willing to dance with the mystery a bit and be influenced by unknown forces, when I'm off for an adventure with only a sketchy map and I open up a little doorway in to that other world, the doorway opens in both directions, and I can be a changing element of meaning in someone else's experience even as they are in mine. As we sit in the lodge each week and pray for an opening into the spirit world, we are also answering prayers. I've been told that the spirits really appreciate us doing these ceremonies, because they cannot do them without us and they love the fire, the prayers, the songs. The openings go both ways.

## Mitakuye Ob Waniktaca

Why do we do these things? Sometimes when I'm struggling with a heavy load of wood and just feeling my brain poaching under that sun, I do think about how much I am willing to do in order to have this ceremony every week. Looking from a stranger's perspective, I say "This must be really important to him."

A friend once remarked that I've chosen an extremely demanding spiritual practice. It struck me a little odd because I don't feel like I chose this practice – it chose me. But she was right. "You can't fake it", she said, "and it's not something you can just do on the spur of the moment." Well that's true. Everything about this practice involves getting out there and working with our neighbors the trees, rocks, earth. Digging holes and building fires, that seems like what we're doing all the time.

For the folks who show up at our lodge every week – or even just more than once – there is something deeply motivating; this is not a casual thing for most people to do even once, and to come back voluntarily seems to me to indicate some degree of dedication. Why? Because it's hard, it's hot. We do these ceremonies in the morning usually, and sometimes we're coming out of the lodge at the hottest part of the day. It's not like North Dakota in January. Well, ok, that's really no picnic either.

So why do we do this? Often it's because we're struggling with a question – which way to go, how to handle a tough situation. Very often it's for healing for ourselves or a loved one. Many times when

I've been visiting family on the Rez, we'd get a call out of the blue "Miles! Please go get that fire started, we're going in, John's uncle is sick and we need to pray for him." Or we come to ask for an easy journey for one who has left this earth. And does that mean we're asking for an easing of our own pain at the loss? Well of course.

We do this for relief from fear, anxiety, depression. To have a sense of family, community, belonging. We do this to open up a little window into the world of mystery, the sacred world of the unknown. Sometimes to ask for impossible healings or divine guidance. Sometimes when I'm just drawing on my Sun Dancer strength to get that last huge log up the hill, it strikes me how very important this is to me – and how this practice calls forth the tenacity, dedication, and strength from wherever it is sourced. How often I've had the sense that I cannot really do this alone, I can't go cut half a cord of wood in the noonday Hawaiian sun and then buck it up and load it, carry it to the lodge, unload it, build a fire, sing the songs.... Yes, there are times when I do all that alone – yet not really alone. The earth does rise up to meet me, the stones and the logs lighten themselves as I carry them. Judy's noticed this so often – she usually carries the stones for our lodge – that the stones will help her and work with her. Really, you should see her carrying these huge heavy lava rocks with such grace, like a dance. They do work with her and all of us feel closer as we experience that. I started calling her "Tunkawan Tanka Ob Waci" – "Dances with Huge Sacred Stones". (the "c" is pronounced like "ch" in "China")

We do these things to be close to our relatives. The earth, the sky, the rock, the grasses. Our families, our friends, our community. Last week as I was cutting and carrying the wood, I just kept hearing "mitakuye ob waniktaca" over and over. It's part of some of the songs we sing, it means "to walk with our relatives" or "I will be walking with my relatives" or "in order to walk with our relatives". It usually is followed by something like "lena cicuelo" – that's why we do these things. I love being out on the land so much. There's a deep pleasure for me in smelling that earth, feeling it beneath me, hearing the birds gossiping in the trees. These trees, the fallen or no longer growing ones we use for the lodge – the spirit has not completely gone out of them, it feels like. They're dead surely, yet they carry something powerful still. All those years out under that sun, working so hard to grow and become strong rising right up out of the rock. How wonderful the power that still inhabits this wood, like sunlight released into the stones in the fire, then breathing upon us in the lodge. As I sit with my relatives in the lodge I give thanks for all of these relationships and the mysterious way that energy and life passes among us.

Later that week I was getting some more wood from a friend I'm doing a trade with, computer help for firewood. At first I was a little reluctant to do this because I love getting the wood so much and don't want to give up doing that. But he and I had such a good time talking and sharing, and being out on the land together loading up the wood – gee, "to be walking with my relatives" and some of them walk on two legs just like I do! I'd almost forgotten – it's not just the rocks and trees that have things to tell me, stories for me to share

Yesterday I was cutting wood again and thinking still about mitakuye ob wani ktaca. I do this because I'm going to be walking with my relatives. This time it feels like I have an obligation to my relatives. You know, it's another angle, another aspect of the same collection of impressions and images and ideas. So thinking about obligation – it was funny because usually if you tell me I'm obligated to do something, right away I'll resist that. But this time it wasn't like that at all. It felt like an exchange, a partnership – that kind of obligation I'm OK with. Like things I do for Judy, it doesn't feel like a burden or really like an obligation – it's just natural. Same with this. This is the obligation that warriors and Sun Dancers have. Walking this path means taking care of the people, making sure the old and sick ones get fed and clothed, helping the children. In the old ways, that's what warriors did when they weren't actually going to war. Carrying these logs and stones, trudging up this hill with this load – it feels so right to be working this hard, because it's the way that's been given to me to do my part for the people. In my capitalist life, I look for an equitable exchange of values, that's what underlies the efforts we put forth when we're free and not enslaved. Now I think of this more as balance – not exactly "I give you this and you give me that", but "I have these abilities and therefore I must use them". Or "I know these songs and therefore I must sing them." I don't bristle at the feeling that my prayers carry an obligation with them. If you're going to sit down and pray for a healing, for understanding or strength or relief of some kind, then of course you are obligated to live inside that prayer.

# Alone As Usual

I am more aware of my solitude today as I wade through the fountain grass to a cluster of kiawe trees that survived – or at least remained standing after – the huge fires that raged along the South Kohala coast last year. We've had a few really heavy rains in the past month and this grass has grown so much it's changed the color and the shape of the hillside.

These trees are so beautiful – 40-foot gently arched trunks, solid and dense. Some have five or six 8-inch thick offshoots from a single base, gnarled and bent by decades of trade winds and storms, having stood through fire and still standing, still firmly anchored in the living rock. A deep crusty brown when they were still alive, now they're smooth and grey, with wide black charred stripes low on the trunks.

Today they seem alone – each one proudly clinging to its chosen pedestal, like us – going through the fire together in a way, sure, but ultimately alone, each on our own unique path. We do these ceremonies together, we come together and greet each other and celebrate this tiyospaye, this extended family. We are walking with our relatives, mitakuye ob wani ktaca. Yet each of us is doing this alone – we come together to do this alone like a family. We can look at each other and see what we see – a strong person, perhaps, a beautiful one. A happy, healthy person – or a sad, struggling one. But you cannot really know what's going on inside from outside.

You could watch me cutting this wood today and think "there's someone who's at peace, at home on the land, doing hard work and evidently satisfied to be doing it", or you could think "what on earth could be driving that poor guy to be out here in the heat of the day on a Saturday with a chainsaw working that hard for that long?" You don't know, looks the same from out there.

You could look at these trees and say "how sad, these once-alive once-strong and rugged kiawe trees just insisting on living and growing right out of this harsh moonscape, and now see how the strong proud ones have withered and died in the fire and the drought", or you might say "how wonderful, these trees still carry so much energy. Even in death, look how much spirit they have, how immensely strong they are still."

So I'm feeling my solitude, and this song is running around me – it says "I'm sending my voice, friend where are you? Where is that one who will help me? Grandfather, where are you?" and I think it's going to be a hard lodge tomorrow.

# Back To My Roots

It was drenching rain yesterday when I went to get the wood. I kept driving, praying, ruminating on some of the difficulties I have at holiday time, and not really thinking too much about the wood. Pretty soon I realized I was almost as far south as another spot where I used to go all the time so I went there. It had been about a year since I'd cut wood at this place, and it looked kind of different. There's been a lot of rain this year and large areas that used to be all brown are now mostly green. I stopped at a place where there's a lot of grey mixed with the green – these kiawe trees turn a beautiful shade of grey when they've stood in the sun for a few years, their bark mostly gone. I walked in about 100 yards over the lava – you have to be careful here, it's much older growth than the place I've been going lately, and there's a lot of underbrush, a lot of saplings too, and there are lava tubes and canyons that are not visible from any distance. Have to watch your step.

I was feeling particularly sad and self-critical yesterday and this place did a lot to calm me. I used to come here to cut wood every week for about 6 years, I've seen it change and move. Less than a hundred years ago this was a swath of completely barren wasteland, burned and then crusted over by earth center-stuff leaving nothing living in its wake. And I have that feeling a little – to lay waste, to explode out and wipe it all away. Yet now, this is a woods of what they call "junk trees" – the hardy and indomitable kiawe that root in the rock and make a life for themselves where you'd say there was no hope. My sister's psychiatrist once said something like that about us after getting a good image of what our childhood was like: "you two just grew like weeds, I don't understand how." So maybe that's part of why I love this place so much.  There are families of goats living here, and birds, spiders, I even saw a jackrabbit once although I had no idea there were any on this island.  Coming back to this familiar powerful place is itself like a ritual, comforting.  As we spiral through life, you know we revisit the same place again and again – but with a different perspective, with something that's been added, subtracted, changed since the last visit.  There's opportunity in that repetition, a chance to take a look at myself and touch something familiar.  Well, that might be sugar-coating it a little – sometimes for me it's an opportunity to beat myself up again, thinking how much I had and have lost since I last stood in this place.  But that's an opportunity too if I can find compassion for that voice of fear and small-s self, separate and alone and afraid.

After a while I realized I had not actually been paying attention to the experience of getting the wood.  Not necessarily the best policy when you're using a chain saw.  I fear my chain saw, and I truly think anyone who doesn't is nuts.  As I walked back into the forest I passed several spots where I could see my own tracks – branches drying in the sun, stumps, pathways through these groves.  There was a tree I recognized, that had 4 low branches all just right, but all with a few green tendrils last time I was here.  I never intentionally take anything living, even if it has just one little branch with a few green leaves on it I don't think it's my place to decide to cut that off.  There are times, of course, when I participate fully in the process of life feeding on life.  I've helped kill a buffalo, I help cut down the Sun Dance tree every year, I don't think groceries originate at the grocery store.  I just don't wantonly increase the death toll when there's no need – there's a wealth of down and standing dead trees here.  But now three of these branches are devoid of any hint of green, they're  brittle and the bark is falling off. It will actually help the tree, part of which is still living, to trim these off – bonus!

Because of the distance back to the truck and the difficulty of the terrain, I try to carry as much as I can in each trip. I don't buck up the wood where I cut it, I carry big branches and trunks up to the road and do it there. As I was struggling slowly under the weight of two of these branches, trying to keep them from cutting into my shoulders, I found myself again bemoaning my fate and feeling alternate self pity and self loathing. Self being the key word, and feeling bad about being alone, yet at the same time feeling so very at home in this place, and a nameless feeling, a kind of animal sense of place, that would not have been the same – is not the same – with others present. So I'm crying out urging myself up the slope to the road with these trees bearing down on my shoulders, and suddenly just for a moment everything cleared up, I stood up straight with no discomfort, I felt the weight of the logs lightening and shifting on their own to a comfortable place, it was like what happens at the Sun Dance when you stop worrying about whether you can do it and you just go out there and dance and make the sacrifice and then it's like there's no "me" for just a moment – all of us are the Dance. And it struck me, that thought, with tears in my eyes and laughing, for just a fraction of a moment, "I am the ceremony, the fire, the wood, the stones, the lodge, I am doing this and being and receiving this, I am that." But even putting it that way is not accurate – there was no "I" in the thought at all. It was more an awareness that the ceremony was proceeding, the wood was being carried, the preparations were underway. All the time I had been busy feeling sorry for myself or whatever I was doing, my body did not stop cutting and carrying the wood, the preparations were continuing as it were without me. Without "me". "Mitakuye Oyas'in" we say, and this moment was that. If I say "taku hwo?" – what is that? "taku" means "what" in that way – yet when my friend Godfrey says something is "taku wakan", it doesn't just mean it's "what is mysterious", it means it's the essence, the core, the "what" of wakan. When we say "mitakuye" it means more than "relatives", it means "I am that", it's a shift of identity – to identify "me" as "that" means to lose track of which is "me" and which is "that", so even saying "I am the ceremony" already separates me from the ceremony.

And the funny thing is, that in that non-moment of oneness, how could I be other than completely alone? You know what I mean? If I am that, then we are all that, and there's nobody home but me. Or that. Thinking that thought sort of broke the mood. Yet in that moment there was a breakthrough, strength had returned, and the rest of the walking, carrying, cutting, unloading, stacking – it was easy. Not effortless, no – the effort was a real pleasure. And the lodge today had that kind of feeling, that kind of pattern to it. The first round was really hot and brought all of us to a place of humility and prayer. The second round was longer and nearly as hot, and towards the end there was a palpable release and everyone seemed to get stronger, the singing voices were clearer and had more of the breath of life in them. As it so often does, the ceremony became an opening for us to experience true gratitude for ourselves, for each other, for the family that we are, for the way of Mitakuye Oyas'in.

That door that we're putting so much into opening up, that little window into the world of mystery – do you see that it is a two-way opening? Once you crack it open, yes, perhaps you can get a taste of Wakan Tanka, and at the same time, that world of mystery gets a taste of you too. We participate in each other's surroundings. And more than that, our consciousness makes a difference – is light a stream of particles or a wave form? It makes a difference what questions we ask and what degree of our consciousness we invest into them. The answers we seek are at least influenced by, if not actually composed of, the questions. Mitakuye Oyas'in.

Woodcuts

## Sometimes It's Just Hard

Last Saturday when I went for the wood, the sun was unchallenged for complete supremacy over the sky and, it seemed, all of life on Earth. Man, it was hot. I had plenty of water and plenty of time and just about enough energy. It is really something what a difference it makes when there's even just a little cloud cover or a breeze. It was an unusually calm day – the trade winds that blow pretty much all the time were taking a break. Too hot, I guess.

So, other than that, it was a very hot day. I mentioned that, right? OK. Well, this is exactly what I was doing then – I was talking to myself, checking out the street and the wind and the ocean and doing everything I could think of other than getting that saw out, putting on my goggles and gloves, grabbing that tobacco and heading into the grove for firewood. Now when I say "grove" please don't hear "rainforest" or even "woods". I'm talking about a few barren, un-barked and un-leaved trees in the middle of a desert. You take three steps, you're sweating already. Hot.

OK, enough. So I got out of the truck and got on with it. And as I trudged down towards the trees, which evidently were not going to cut themselves and stack themselves up by the road, I looked for a silver lining – a story, a lesson, a balancing uplifting gift of some kind to relieve the unalloyed agony. Nothing was forthcoming. I sang my songs, which usually infuses me with energy, but really it didn't help. My legs were aching, I was panting and sweating and really struggling.

And you know, it's really something – I was not bummed, honestly. I was truly amazed at the absence of the familiar feelings of guilt, shame, depression, self-doubt, self-recrimination --- none of the above! I was without any serious thoughts or feelings other than the physical striving and you know what? It was just hard. Not wonderful, no – I wanted to turn this into some kind of inspirational thing, but it wasn't. It was just hard.

Well the next day in the lodge one of our regulars was having a pretty difficult time, and I shared this story of the wood, intending not really to cheer her up but just to say – sometimes there's nothing for it but to go through it, it's just hard. And then, then there was a shift of meaning or interpretation – because then, as I intended to share my misery with her I realized that this friend, like me, has a tendency to load up the moment with baggage from the past and I heard, not aloud and not really in words, "Sometimes it's just hard. It's not punishment. It's not the final embodiment of your wasted life and tragic failure as a human being. It's just hard."


Ah.

# Inner Tree, Outer Tree

Last week I went to a different spot to get wood, about half a mile from the usual place. The wood's been getting farther and farther from the road and I was a bit tired that day, looking for something a little easier. I parked and started walking in towards a small stand of dead trees about 150 yards across a relatively flat lava field. Just as I got down to the flat, not 30 feet from the road, I took another look at a tree I'd decided to leave alone because it had so much green. I don't take anything living for these fires. Well, as I looked again I saw a tree within the tree. Kiawe grows that way, all tangled and wound around, and here was a live tree with a dead one coming right up out of the middle of it. As it happened, the angle I approached from, I was looking into the sun behind the tree. Gee, this is familiar. Standing looking up at the sun and a tree. At our Sun Dance we do one of the days at night. After dancing all day gazing at the sun, we dance all night gazing at the moon. It's like being in a photographic negative – the blazing sun is now the cold moon, the dark tree is now bright, the blue-white sky is now black. Standing there on the lava field, looking at the sun, looking at the live tree and the dead one superimposed – it was like my name and address were clearly printed on the envelope. OK, I'm in! So I took a closer look and saw that with a few cuts I could extract that dead tree without harming the live one, and it would actually be better for the tree to get trimmed in that way, to clear its space out.

So I made those cuts – one of them, I knew, would bring a large branch down on top of me. I did it, stepped aside and killed the saw as it fell, and was not hurt at all. I thought, there are lots of ways to experience the same experience! I mean, I could be saying "Man! What a tough day! The sun right in my eyes while I'm trying to cut, this tree all tangled up with live branches, and one of them just came right down on me!"

The branches fell away in the four directions, it was really beautiful. It reminded me of one of the most moving parts of the Sun Dance, something a firekeeper would know about, but even the dancers might not. The fire at the Sun Dance is kept burning night and day for the whole 4 days. It cannot go out – if that fire goes out, the Sun Dance is over. So when you're firekeeper, either you get a lot of help or you don't get a lot of sleep. At the end of the four days, there's a wonderful symbolic gift given by one of the pure young girls of the tribe, a gift that reminds us of the way we were first given these sacred ceremonies. And as that is unfolding, the firekeeper is slowly taking the fire apart, dropping the remaining logs out in the four directions, so that when the ceremony ends, the fire is out.

Anyway, I took down that tree, and prayed thanks for the life it had led. And thanks for the easy time collecting wood this week – it was really just what I needed, I'd been having a pretty rough time internally and didn't feel up to a very strenuous journey. Although, when I go for the wood that's when the ceremony begins for me and no matter what's going on I always feel strengthened and supported by the earth, the grass, the birds, the stones, the trees, sky, ocean ... all my relatives.

So I got a great load of wood – about enough for two lodges. It took half the time it usually does, and was so much easier. Wow. Sometimes it's just easy!

# Which Way Will It Fall?

Cutting the wood yesterday I moved down further into the ravine I've been gathering from. There was a good looking tree just at the edge of an even deeper little valley. I eyeballed it carefully and made the cut so that it would fall uphill and not down where it would be harder to get out. It fell just where I aimed it and I was feeling pretty good about that. Wondering what message, what gift there might be in this for my family, I remembered two years ago at the Sun Dance – all of us were out getting the tree. Some of the men had tied their ropes to help guide it down – when we cut this tree we do not allow it to hit the ground – and looking at it I could see it was going to fall the opposite way from they way they were expecting. I looked around, no one said anything, and I didn't either. Now I know that if I can really get completely underneath and inside myself in that moment of not speaking, I can learn something important. Why didn't I speak up?

In the first moment when I looked at the tree I knew which way it was going to fall. Cutting with an axe as we were, not a chainsaw which I use in my weekly ceremony, you have a lot less control over the direction it'll fall. I've cut down a lot of trees, and seen how they fall and how they lean. I've had a chainsaw stuck fast in a big tree trunk because despite my angled cuts it fell the way it wanted to and jammed my saw in the cut. My eye remembered those lessons and I knew.

In the next moment I was thinking about what everyone else there must be thinking. Surely there are many others here who would know if the tree was going to fall the other way. Surely with all these Sun Dancers and highly experienced singers, water pourers, the Old Man –

well, I'm just outnumbered. Surely they know and it would be presumptuous of me to butt in.

In the next moment I was advising myself to be humble, to remember that I don't live on the Rez, I'm the white guy from Hawaii. Actually nobody looks at me that way, it's my own insecurity. The guy from Hawaii, yes – they call me "Hawaii Dave". But nobody on this reservation has ever given me any flak at all about being white. One of my friends said to me "you're not wasicun" when I said something about being one. So here is the truth emerging – I made all this stuff up in the moments after the initial natural knowing told me what was going to happen.

And it gets more complicated too. For quite a while in my life I was pretty much always the first one to speak up whenever there was a question to be answered – whether I had a clear answer or not. Then I got a lot of feedback about that, and the pendulum swung the other way – I would purposely keep quiet even when I really had something to contribute. I told myself I was being polite or something – letting someone else have the chance to speak first and make that contribution. But then it changed its appearance to me – I began to think this was really a form of arrogance: "I have the answer, and I'm so wonderful that I don't need to be the one to speak it, someone else can take the credit, because I'm just that huge a person." Which I suppose might be true in someone else with a different attitude, but for me it was arrogant. And also, in many cases, it meant that our group or team or company didn't progress as fully or rapidly as we might have if I'd shifted my focus off myself and onto our shared goal.

Well, that tree fell back towards my friends who were prepared with their ropes to slow down its fall in the other direction, and we who were waiting to catch it watched helplessly while it crashed down at frightening speed directly opposite where we were standing. No one was hurt, which is incredible, and we made a joke about it – too many heyokas in this tribe! – but boy, did I feel crappy. Talking about it afterwards I found out that there were several of us who had the same thought – "that tree is going to fall the other way" – and none of us spoke up. For different reasons? Maybe, but we are all related.

The following week I was down in the same ravine about 20 feet away, working on another tree that was leaning over the crevasse, and I said to myself "no problem, I'll just have this fall uphill like the other one, I'm good at that". Bashi! they say in Japanese. Hubris. Well, I made the cut just right and the tree fell just in the direction I wanted it to ... and its top got caught up in another tree right next to it, the base slid out and hit the ground, and the tree sprung back and landed right on me. Scratched up my arm pretty good, no other damage.

And I thought about the next year, I was dancing, and one of my friends asked me to help him. He'd seen how I completed my vow that year and thought it was strong, and he wanted me to support him. Well, at one point what he really needed was a drill sergeant, he needed me to be very forceful and just insist that he do what he needed to do. And I just couldn't do it. I froze up. Not for long, I went and got help from one of the more experienced dancers, a relative of the man I was trying to help, and together the two of us supported him and it was all good. But – why did I freeze up?

I have in my not-too-distant past been a real jerk, know-it-all, power-play kind of guy. So here's another pendulum swing – in breaking the habit of being devastatingly hostile when all that was really called for was assertiveness, I pulled inward, afraid to fall into that black pit of rage, not knowing how to be strong, firm, stand my ground, even to push someone hard with love.

These opposites keep teaching me. In the lodge we are in the midst of a great clash of opposites. The cold water on the red-hot stones. The air and the fire. The earth and the stone. The darkness and the firelight. The four directions, the heaven and the earth. Flesh and spirit, matter and energy. So what can I do, but keep going? Keep praying, try next time to give my friend what he really needs from me, try to trust my knowing what that is, be willing to make a mistake by acting rather than retreating. Did our people learn these lessons hundreds of years ago doing this ceremony? I think so – but without all these words.

## Fly South

Building the fire today, I had trouble getting the stones to balance and pile up. You've never seen me do this, so you don't know how unusual this is – normally I don't give it any thought at all, I just build the fire and it takes its own shape, each one different. Well, today it just kept going wonky in one way or another. I'd get the 10th stone on there and the 6th and 7th would topple off, things like that. Once the west stone toppled down and cracked me in the leg, ouch. Well finally I got them all to balance. There were three in the south that looked like they were trying to escape, they were leaning over so far. But I figured, OK, well I'll just place the logs around as usual and they'll stay in place. Then I took a step towards the pile of dry grass, and about 4 stones tumbled out of the pile onto the floor of the pit.

All right, I get it already! I took the whole thing apart and started over again. Doing that, I realized that I was kind of grumbling to myself about it so I stopped and stepped away from the sacred circle for a moment. Whenever I'm doing any part of this ceremony – cutting the wood, building the fire, anything – I don't hold anger or bad feelings towards anyone, including myself – just remain in a state of prayer as much as possible. Naturally there's a bit of drift and it's not like I'm constantly monitoring myself or struggling to stay cool, it's just that when I do catch a sour thought I take a moment. So I did that, and doing so I realized how funny! I didn't really pray at all while building this fire. I mean, I went through the motions, but I was really not there. So I started all over again and when I got to the south and prayed for life, health, generations, I realized I had skipped this completely the first time around. I got to the lodge early this morning, determined to have the stones ready by 9am when we ask people to arrive. I didn't want to keep them waiting. So there I was rushing through the building of the fire, silly boy, and having to start all over again. And really, what's the problem anyway? These are not things that we do on "clock time", we do them in their own time.

Well I put that fire together the second time and it was really good, a solid pile of stones, the fire came right up with one match and the stones were good and red at 9 o'clock. The first round was really toasty, I think we did 2 or 3 songs after the opening prayer. We had a new person in there with us, and the moment we opened that door, out she flew. She had been sitting in the south, and she got out of the lodge, out of the circle, and went right home. I think she was gone before the steam stopped rising out of the door. Now that woman is our relative. We are compassionate towards her – we know how hot it is in there, especially for someone who's not used to it. So we want her to come back. It would be different if there had been no energy around it, but there was quite a bit. She called us during that week, saying she just found it much too harsh, not what she had known years ago when she did these ceremonies with someone in California. There, they just brought in 4 stones at a time and got them good and cold before bringing in any more.

Well, we don't want it so hot that people can't pray. Yet if we make it so comfy that there's no challenge, nothing much is going to get done. A long time ago I stopped trying to know or be in control of how hot or long the rounds are. That may sound a bit odd since I'm building the fire, putting the stones into it, pouring the water on them, calling for the door. If I'm not in control, who is? Right? That's a big question. For me it has been wonderfully valuable to come to the realization that I am not running the show – that there are substantial events and forces affecting my life that I do not understand or cause. Does this mean that there is someone else who *is* running the show? I don't think so. I think it's just running, and we're all part of it. It's a delicate balance for me, to be present and pay attention to how everyone is doing, to pour the water and sing the songs – to be the physical mechanism for carrying out the "doing" of the ceremony – and at the same time to be a participant, one who is taking part in the unfolding of this lodge at this time with these stones and these people. If I try to shorten it because I think someone's having a hard time, or lengthen it because I think someone needs more prayer, well then I'm getting in the way and making judgments where that's not what's called for. Yet at the same time I don't relinquish my judgment, do I? I am, after all, paying attention to how people are doing, and there's a judgment involved in answering that question. So what I do is, I try to keep this as simple as possible. I'm in there, we're all in there together, and really anyone can call for the door at any time, they know that. I try to give whatever I'm receiving right away as it comes to me. That way I don't get all confused about control and judgment and who needs what, I just allow myself to flow along with the stones and the water and the steam.

So we want this woman to come back, because something drew her to the ceremony in the first place, and then something pushed her away. And that was not a "just so, who cares?" kind of fact for her – she spoke to a few of us afterwards about how hot it was and how it was not what she was expecting, and not they way they do it in California. So there's still something there available for her to receive, you see? As long as there's an argument or a justification, an explanation, a sort of apology – then there's something else operating besides the surface facts. Call it what you like – a spirit, an archetype, an unconscious constellation – there's something there. When you find yourself flying south, look north.

## Who Is "I"?

Yesterday I went back to that valley where the Ironman tree took me. From the rim I saw a pair of trees about 30 feet tall, looked like a good diameter. I hesitated because I knew it was going to be tough climbing up out of there with those trees on my back. There's another spot not too far from there, a longer hike back to the truck but flatter land. I was there a couple of weeks ago and I know there are some branches on the ground there that I can use. I stood right there for a little while wondering which way to go. Unusual for me – I normally just walk in, pick a spot, and start cutting. It's been my thought that "spirit" is the aspect of consciousness that chooses. So if I'm pondering two different choices, what's going on? Is my spirit undecided? That doesn't sound right. Am I having trouble hearing my spirit, or differentiating the "true" choice from a false one? Closer, I think. Whenever we're on the horns of a dilemma, doesn't that question lie under the subject matter? How to know which voice is the true spirit, which is the devil on my left shoulder or the angel on my right? They both sound so certain, so unconditionally right – which is pretty much what "dilemma" means, now that I think of it. Two premises, two underlying assumptions. It occurs to me that back in the days before ceremonies, when the people just lived naturally, there was probably not a whole lot of thinking about thinking. These different ideas might arise, but I would imagine that their source was mysterious. Maybe this is what was meant by having the spirits talking to you. Imagine what it would be like if you didn't have any understanding of thinking itself – didn't know where these ideas came from or even necessarily identify them as your own thoughts.

Well as you can imagine, at this point I had to laugh and say to myself "OK, unless you're planning on heating up those stones with red-hot ideas about primitive consciousness, you'd better pick a direction and start cutting."

I chose the valley, walked down there and as I approached I realized that the trees were a lot skinnier than they looked from up top. Oh well. But just a few yards away was another clump that was just perfect. So I walked over there, thinking about voices and spirits in your head. We all hear voices, really, don't we? I mean, we think about what's going to happen or what has happened, we rehearse what we're going to say or we replay previous conversations. We compose better lines for ourselves, right? Am I the only one who does that? Aren't these all ways of being elsewhere? What if I just settle down into the present moment?

Well this is an odd thing. As I considered that I started to feel guilty – it's a strange thing, but there's a kind of process I notice inside me that is reluctant to relax and be present in the moment, because in some way it feels like I'm denying the truth of how terribly I've screwed up, how much I have to struggle now because of the mistakes I've made. I feel guilty. And as that arose I actually heard this, even said it out loud: "Guilty? No, I don't feel guilty, why should I? You're finally starting to pay attention to me. I understand that *you* feel guilty – it's ok, you made a lot of really bad choices and spent an awful lot of energy justifying them. But you were also looking for me the whole time and trying to find a way to trust my voice without faking anything or just giving up on being certain. And that insistence, that stubbornness – that's a real asset that we share."

I could feel a shift inside me as I listened to that voice – for a moment, a few minutes, I was free of recrimination and guilt. I didn't even feel the recrimination I often focus on that inner critic that's so full of guilt-generating observations – which for me is a real trap, an alternate way of leveling brutal criticism against myself. No, for this space of time we were in relationship: that frightened, rather desperate one inside me and that wise, patient, enduring one. What responds when you say "I" – that self-identification – that was in a different place for a while. And as I cut that wood – for I notice that even as I dance these inner mental dances I keep on cutting and carrying the wood – as I worked I noticed that I was really, really strong. I carried hundreds of pounds of hard, dense kiawe wood up a really steep incline – not quite a ladder but a lot more than a flight of stairs – and didn't give any thought to bargaining ("I'll just take one more load after this one."). I just cut and carried that wood, bucked it up, loaded it in the truck. There's a concordance of spirit and body, isn't there, when you stop fighting yourself and find that relationship? This is part of what "inipi" really means, the strengthening of that inner breath of living spirit.

## Ask And Ye Shall Receive

Yesterday I stopped at a new spot – a little tougher to get down to the wood, but what a beautiful supply there is! I was struck by the beauty and the solitude of this brush-covered lava field. Just 10 feet from the road, with cars zipping by, yet I bet none of those people saw me or noticed what was going on just out of their angle of view.

So I strolled carefully down that incline, balancing my body and my focus too, between the path ahead and the ocean and sky around me. And I said "OK, let's have a story!" and laughed because it seemed a little impertinent – and yet, that's really how I hope you are feeling as you turn these pages, and I was sort of mirroring that attitude towards the unknown source of these stories. Now there's a mind-bender. You're reading this after I am writing it, obviously. And yet your attitude while you're reading it is influencing my attitude before I wrote it. Bzzzt!

Anyway – so I did, I asked for a story. I started to say "I'm open to a story", but really that didn't express it. I really meant "Please, tell me a story now". So that's what I said. "Ask", or "be open to" – that can be a tricky one. Judy says the exercise of free will and causality is what happens when you decide to pray for a particular outcome. I like that – it expresses the scope of our free will beautifully. Even Ayn Rand said that volition comes down to a single fundamental choice: to be conscious or not. She certainly didn't mean "to pray or not", but that's a different conversation. I think she was actually referring to the same phenomenon that Judy's talking about – we have a choice to participate consciously in the great swirl of life unfolding, to exert what influence we can on the outcomes of events. And *that* is the difference between "I'm open to" and "please". If you tell me you're open to having me wash your car – well, how nice for you to be so open. Openness is good. Do you see me washing your car? Now, if you were to ask me to wash your car – well, at least you'd have a better chance of having that happen. You'd have made your choice to influence the outcome – and then events not under your control occur, and maybe I wash your car and maybe not. That's how prayer is.

The important part of all this is what goes on inside of you in the praying, or the asking, or the being open. At one time it may be that what's true for you is that you are open to a particular outcome. If you're not in a place to ask for it directly yet you're OK with it happening, there you are. But if you're really wanting to have that outcome happen, well, I say ask for it. Learning to ask for what we want can be a tremendous opening for some of us who have had lots of difficult experiences with asking and being refused.

As I pondered this I was balancing some really impressive tree parts on my shoulders and lugging them up the hill. This land requires that I keep a large part of my energy and focus right directly on the path in front of me. If I wander too far afield, mentally, I can easily step on a loose rock or hit an incline at a bad angle, and with all that extra weight it's no fun. Yet when I finish with a train of thought and just go quiet, it's like I'm gliding up that hill, so smoothly that I don't really know what's happening until afterwards when I come out of that state of thoughtlessness and notice the huge pile of wood I've got ready for cutting and loading. And it occurs to me that when I'm really trying to stay balanced, the only part of me that's out of balance is the part that's trying to stay balanced. Gah! Fortune cookie! But really, it's true.

The last limb I was carrying was really twisted and curled around – it's the way these trees grow, wrapped around each other and bent by the wind. "Miksuye" came to me for some reason – "Remember". My first teacher said that the only thing the mind is really good for is memory. To remember the songs, the lessons, the way home, how to build the fire. Now I'm not sure I agree with him on that, but remembering is unquestionably handy. Miksuye. The first time I heard that word was when someone said "Miksuye Cankpe Opi" – Remember Wounded Knee. It's a reminder of the terrible killing that happened there in December 1890, that we should never forget the blindness, cruelty, brutality that is possible for human beings. And in our pipe-filling song we sing "miksuye opagiyo" – remember to make a prayer offering. When you carry a pipe, when you make an altar, remember to pray. How funny and how wonderful, I thought, that we sing this prayer song while filling the pipe, and the song reminds us to pray. Well, I got to the top of the hill and leaned over to drop that limb onto the pile and one of those curled branches just caught me from behind the knees and dropped me right down onto a rock, on my knees. It didn't do any damage but it sure got my attention. Wounded knee? Not today, thanks. "What?" – oh my, I got it in that moment. In all my enthusiasm for a story I had actually forgotten to pray! First time I've done that. I always begin with a tobacco offering, and ask them to watch over me while I do this dangerous work, and to watch over everyone who comes to our lodge, and all those who cannot or will not come to a ceremony like this – watch over them and their families and take care of them. I give thanks for the spirit of these standing wood people and invite them to join me, to help us do this ceremony, to yield up their energy to the stones and go on to the next place. But not today! So I thanked that tree and that rock, and tried to get up.

Couldn't do it, I'm telling you, that tree had me good and pinned down. So ok, I fished my tobacco pouch out and made the offering right there, said a good long prayer of thanks and asked for help for myself and my family and those I knew about who were in need of some support. *Miksuye opagiyo,* yeah. And if you forget, the trees will remember.

Now, I'm hearing you say "asked *them*? Who's 'them'?" OK – fair question. I did claim to be rational and a nonbeliever, and here I am talking about praying and asking for various things, so what exactly is going on with that? Well – it appears to me that life is a deeply complex interconnected flow. We affect each other and the world around us not only by the things we plan and do, but also by subtle attitudes, fortuitous choices, many things we're not usually conscious of. Furthermore, I know that my state of health and wellbeing is affected by my attitude, by my conscious intentions as well as those that are not so conscious. So, to pray is to place myself intentionally into a particular state of mind, a state of focus. I'm letting my cells know how I want things to be, and I'm letting my less-than-fully-conscious self know too. We make choices by the thousands, every minute of the day, and we don't give our conscious attention to more than a tiny fraction of them. One of the things I think about prayer is that it's a way to set a context for the rest of them. How these choices affect us internally or externally is mysterious and I don't pretend to understand it. That there is an effect, though, seems very clear to me.

So, prayer is a way to remember, a way to honor the request *miksuye opagiyo,* a way to unify the conscious, subconscious, physical, emotional parts that I call "me".

## Fire Keeper

This morning it was raining as I drove to the lodge site to get the fire going. Not a little sprinkle, I'm talking about a real driving rain with big drops and splashes. So of course I started praying, asking for just a little opening there for me to get the fire going. Once it's started, it's not that hard to keep it going and get the stones heated up even in a pretty good rain. But starting it under water is hard work. Well here's another of those dances – we've had this experience so many times over the years it's just beyond coincidence. Over and over again I've been in this situation, and I pray sincerely and ask for just what I need – not an end to all rain, not an interruption of the gift that this rain is for the land – just a small opening so I can get the fire started. And I'm telling you, it almost always happens. Sometimes just a brief letup, enough to get it going. Sometimes, more often actually, a little hole opens up right above the lodge. It's raining all around but not on the fire pit. So it's a dance – I don't want to be cocky or presumptuous, yet at the same time I have had this experience over and over again, something miraculous happens that enables us to have our ceremony. So I pray for it. Have I experimented with not praying? Well, no, actually I haven't. What would be the point? I did try that once with a different situation and it didn't work, I didn't get the result I was asking for until I sincerely prayed. But I'm not trying to prove anything, I'm trying to get the stones hot. And anyway, how could I do the experiment? I truly do sincerely want this fire to happen, that's what I'm doing out here in the rain. I can't pretend that's not what I'm up to.

Still, this is kind of a challenge for a left-brain atheist rational guy, you know? I mean, what the heck is going on here? It is way, way too consistent to be random chance. Like this morning – I got to the spot where our lodge is, and it was raining. I had the load of firewood in the back of the truck under a plastic tarp, and it was raining on the tarp. I slipped a few logs out and carried them over to the fire pit, thinking I'd slip them under the tarps there where the woodpile is, and then make an enclosure if need be. Well. What can I tell ya? It was not raining on the fire pit. 30 feet away at the truck, rain. Fire pit, dry. I looked up and the sky was all dark clouds. I just kept on praying, unloaded everything and built the fire as usual.

How is this possible? If I were you I'd be asking myself "Is he making this up? Is he just forgetting all the times that the rain didn't stop? Is he somehow lost in his own illusion?" I don't blame you. All I can say is, it really happens. A LOT.

So how could this be? I have actually given some thought to that, from the cause-and-effect standpoint. Weather is a chaotic system, we know it's intensely complex and even though we've gotten pretty good at predicting general patterns, the specific weather conditions in a given small area like my fire pit are the result of such an astronomical swirl of initial conditions and subsequent influences that, while not entirely random, they are beyond calculation. Furthermore, very tiny shifts in atmospheric pressure, electromagnetic conditions like sunspots, wind, earth surface temperature, and any number of other factors can affect the specific nature and amount of precipitation at a given time and place. So why not an intensity of mind-body-spirit focused on a very small area? Absurd?

OK, what about from a non-causal perspective?  Maybe I just am somehow in tune with nature, and I happen to be building the lodge fire just when the rain is letting up, but neither is causing the other.  Perhaps both events are caused by some deeper factor unknown to me, something that accounts for the patterns of rain and sun over the fire pit and that also influences how long it takes me to drag myself out of bed every Sunday morning.  But you see I do this every week at the same time, so it's not just that it happens to be when the rain is going to stop.

And what could prayer have to do with it?  When it comes to my own body, I have an easier time understanding or at least imagining the effect of prayer.  Our state of consciousness obviously affects our bodies – some of us sweat when we're nervous or blush when we're embarrassed.  Ask any really good poker player if there's a mind-body connection – they can read your excitement, fear, disappointment with uncanny accuracy.  So I can see that placing my consciousness into a state of receptivity, focusing on a particular healing or shift that I truly desire without inner contradiction, could bring about or at least lay the groundwork for that very outcome.  But rain letting up?

Does it really matter how this is possible?  Actually to me it does, and I will doubtless keep pondering it for who knows how long.  But no, it really doesn't matter – the point is to get the stones heated for the ceremony.  That's what the fire is doing there.  I've been working with this fire every week for over 12 years.  Every week those stones get red hot.  I've noticed that no matter what else is going on in my life or in the weather conditions, however difficult it may be (and believe me, sometimes it is very difficult) I never wonder "is this fire going to come up at all?".  Many times I look at the woodpile and I know there's not enough wood there to heat up these stones, I know it, I have enough experience to be able to see that. Or sometimes the wood is wet, the dry grass isn't dry, the ground is wet, it's drizzling – it's not reasonable to think a fire will come up blazing in these conditions. Yet I just never wonder "gee, should I give up on it this week?" This is not something I decide prior to heading there, it just seems to be an "of course" for me. I'm there to do the physical work of building the fire and tending it. But somehow it's not "my" fire – I do my part and it does its. So there really is no question of giving up – I don't have anything to give up, rather I'm in a process of discovery – "how is this particular fire going to show up?" And the years I've been doing this make a difference of course. When I say "I've been working with this fire for 12 years", that makes sense, right? It's not this same fire that's been burning for 12 years. I light a new one every week. Yet it is the same fire that's been burning for I don't know how many thousands of years. It's the *inipi* fire, the Sun Dance fire, the *peta owihankesni* – the fire that does not go out. Are you sensing the mysterious nature of this fire? There is the particular burning flame that arises each week when I stack up the stones and logs and light it. And there is what I've been working with for 12 years. One is an instance, the other is a symbol. The particular instance is available to consciousness, the fullness of the symbol is unconscious and imbues the particular with a kind of power. If not for the history and broad context of the *inipi* fire, each weekly fire would not have the meaning it does – and without that context perhaps the fire would not actually come up at all, perhaps something in my attitude or the countless prevailing conditions would be different, and I'd be unable to get the fire started.

If you have a problem with that word "unconscious", as I certainly do, it may help to look at it this way: *Conscious* is to *unconscious* as *cola* is to *uncola*. It's not a kind of consciousness – 7Up is not a kind of Coke. The unconscious is NOT conscious. It's all that other stuff. Symbols, as Jung describes them, live in the interface between those two worlds and draw our attention to what lies beyond the portal.

This morning as I was building the fire, giving thanks for this little window of dryness, I thought about all the times I've seen it come blazing up without enough wood, without enough dry grass, without all the "right" conditions. So many times it's felt to me that I'm not really the one making this fire, I'm just playing my part. In the old times when the people traveled from winter camp to summer camp, following the buffalo, there were a few who had the responsibility of carrying the fire from one camp to the next. These were the firekeepers. They kept burning coals going inside hollowed-out stumps, replenished them as necessary during the trip, so that when the band arrived at their next site they'd be able to get all the family fires started from that one source and not have to go through the arduous task of starting one up from scratch. And I mean "from scratch". The only time they would start a new one would be if some great event or disaster occurred, either some terrible mishap that put out the coals, or some other event that made the people decide to leave that fire on purpose and start up a new one, a new chapter for their band. Either way, it was a big deal and not something you'd want to do very often.

As I was getting the fire going this morning I wondered to myself how this happens, for truly I do not feel like I'm causing the fire. I am participating in it, and playing a vital role, but when you see a fire come blazing up out of wet wood sitting on wet ground with wet grass woven into it – or when you see a bone-dry stack of logs with a bushel of crackly dry grass just refuse to ignite – you have to wonder, ok, what other forces are at work here? So I was having these thoughts and I imagined a conversation among the ones who really do bring up the fire – these metaphorical guardians of the ancient fire. And they were saying "We really have to let him work a little more on this. If we just pop that fire to life now, he'll know for sure it's impossible and it'll freak him. Let him get enough material together and put in enough effort so his cause-effect thing is satisfied and he won't go all ga-ga when the blaze starts up."

At the Sun Dance, someone is responsible for keeping that fire burning during the entire four days and nights, rain or shine. These are the firekeepers. Their responsibility is serious – if the fire goes out, the ceremony is over, and if that happens before all the dancers have fulfilled their commitments, it is a terrible and sad event. One year it rained day and night for 2 days – I was a firekeeper that year. We had to build up a platform of stones in the fire pit because it was filling up with water, and we dug drainage canals to direct the streams away from the tipis and the fire. None of us got much sleep that year – dancers or firekeepers. For me, and I think for all of us, this was a gigantic community effort. No one wondered "maybe we should just stop and try doing this ceremony another time". We just all kept on doing and kept on praying and being carried along by the "of course" of this, even as we put out every available drop of energy to have it continue.

We don't do this just so that we can dance and perform this particular ceremony. We don't do our weekly inipi just for the sake of that one Sunday morning ritual.  When the going is rough, when it's unclear how we're going to have the strength or the wherewithal to complete the task, something much older and deeper is at work that keeps us going, something that is symbolized by but never fully illuminated by what we use and embody. Something in the ancient and eternal quality of this fire and this ceremony perpetuates itself in our "of course".  And that is truly a mystery – in fact, if you look deeply at it you will see that it is The Great Mystery, *Wakan Tanka*.

## Mind Control

Yesterday cutting the wood I was particularly careful walking up and down the rocky slope, singing one of our songs and carrying the cut trees. There was something in my mood that just prompted me to be extra conscious, extra careful about where I placed my energy. Years ago I was embroiled in a difficult conflict with people I had trusted, who turned out to be unworthy of that trust. They were costing me a small fortune in legal fees and I had a hard time maintaining any compassion for them. I kept telling myself "put your energy where it will do some good", and that helped me to think less about them and more charitably. Why should I? you may well ask. If they're doing me harm, purposely, why should I think well of them or wish them well? Why, in other words, should we pray for our enemies?

"While you carry this pipe, you are carrying it for the people, not for yourself", my first teacher told me. "Never use this ceremony to do any harm to anyone. Only health and help, that's all." He told me that while carrying the pipe I must not think angry or harmful thoughts about anyone.

Now that is a tall order. I mean really, think about that – how can you prevent yourself from having an angry thought? If someone has done you wrong or injured your family in some way, don't you get angry? I surely do. And don't you think about getting even, or just have thoughts about how bad that person is, or at least how bad their action is? So how can you possibly not have those thoughts?

As I carry that wood every week, I notice changes in my strength and balance, and these changes often correspond with changes in my mood. This is, I think, one of many ways in which consciousness affects the body – we take it for granted in the case of an athlete, for example, that if she's having personal problems her game is naturally affected by them. This applies very broadly, in my experience. I am actually physically stronger and have greater endurance when my inner life is not in turmoil. When my energy is not being dissipated and divided up among different inner demands. Yesterday that showed up very clearly in my strength – I cut a really good load of wood, heavy and solid, and did it in a fairly continuous effort from start to finish. That's unusual; I ordinarily take a few breaks for breath and water during the woodcutting. Yesterday I was very aware of my thoughts and feelings as I was cutting the wood – something is awakening in me of late, something I remember from nearly 40 years ago, the first time I moved to New York City. I was in a cab going up 6th Avenue from Houston St, and the driver was doing about 50 over this horrible stretch of road, full of potholes and bumps. Something kind of clicked in me, and I felt like I was riding this cab, riding it like an unbroken steer, riding it like a cowboy – and I thought "I'm going to be fine here. I'm going to ride this city like I'm riding this cab." And I did, too, it was a great time for me. Well, that same feeling came through me yesterday as I was cutting the wood, just a sense of being in the right place and with all the resources I need. You can focus on the bumps, on the loose stones and the blazing sun, the grinding weight of the wood. Or you can focus on the excellent soles of your boots, the strength of your limbs, the balance of your body, the feeling of being carried along by this strong and dedicated man.

Do you hear what is shifting inside me? With a prayerful attention to the inner world (I suppose this would be called meditation) it becomes less and less automatic to identify with your thoughts. Instead of the awareness being, for example, "those awful people deserve to be ...", instead the awareness moves to "I am having a vindictive thought about those people". And sometimes, eventually, the awareness is "I am about to have a vindictive thought, let me make a different choice". In the first instance, when the awareness is "those people are X", I am actually identifying with the thought – that is, "I" am embodied in that angry thought, it feels like a fact to me, not something to be considered or evaluated, just a fact to which I am reacting with feelings of anger and pain. No choice in that. But if I am to carry this pipe in the way I've been taught, I need to find a way to get underneath those thoughts and have different ones – and in the process of doing that, I begin to see myself differently. Whatever it is that responds when I say "I" is shifting.

This does not seem to be something that answers to ego control. I've tried, it just doesn't work, you can't simply declare "I will now cease having angry thoughts about those thieving liars" and expect your emotions and your subconscious to obey. But to place yourself into an attitude of prayer involves an opening to something else other than the ego, other than the familiar "I". (You know that "ego" is just the Latin word for "I", right? When Freud and Jung and Adler were talking about this they called it "I" in German first, only later in Latin. "Ich", they called it, and I think that probably conveyed the sense of it to the German reader much more accurately than "ego" does to the English reader. Anyway, what I'm referring to is the conscious, aware, self that usually is referred to by the word "I".) So, what else is there to be open to, that's not some external God or spirit? All I can say is, take a look.

As I was building the fire this morning, it occurred to me that there's way too much thinking going on. I don't know if that was about me, or if I was reflecting on the people who were coming, or what. I did catch myself wondering how many stones to use and trying to predict the different effects on the people who were coming. I stopped that and just followed my instinct as usual. This fire came up like a dream, it was amazing. A single very old kitchen match, kind of soft and not quite damp, it didn't even light up the whole way, but when it touched that dry grass the fire just took off. And then I walked away from it – not my usual habit. Usually I tend the fire for a while, make sure it's burning evenly on all sides, make sure all the stones are covered. Today I left it alone, went and worked on another part of the ceremony that needed attention. And this struck a note in resonance with yesterday's – on the subject of control. If I want to stop having angry thoughts, my first impulse is to exercise more control over my thinking – because the "I" who wants to stop having these thoughts really thinks he's in control, or could be, or should be. Just like I think I am in control of the fire, or should be. That I am responsible for tending it and nurturing it and having it be a certain way. And obviously to a degree that's true – if I didn't come out here every Sunday morning and start it, there'd be no fire, no ceremony. But to what extent is my tending and caring serving the fire, and to what extent serving my beliefs? How much control do I really have over how this fire progresses? And how much difference does it make whether I exercise that control, or just let it progress as it wants to?

Yesterday on the way home from another outing, before I went to cut the wood, it was pouring drenching rain along most of the road home. I was thinking about what I wrote last week, about building the fire in the rain and the whole dance of control and receptivity. How ironic, I thought, I wonder if I'm going to have nothing but wet wood this week. I was imagining going out in the rain and cutting the wood, building the fire in the rain. And I was thinking I would go ahead and do that, rather than not have the ceremony. I want to be open to how it unfolds, to learn from the relaxation of control (or the illusion of control). So I was bravely thinking I'd do my part no matter what the conditions. And as it turned out, it wasn't raining at all in the area where I've been going for wood. So in fact it was relatively easy to gather a sufficient load, and this morning same thing – it was raining here at my house but not where the lodge is, and building the fire and getting it started was easy and smooth. And I realized that being willing to be present for and open to however life might unfold also means being willing to accept it when things are going really well. This is something I have difficulty with. I tend to remember how things used to be, or be fearful about how they might be, and it's an effort sometimes to relax and enjoy a good run of luck, an easy task, a day of no work. Or I just have a hard time seeing myself as innocent and free and happy. It's getting easier, but it's still rough. And as this fire spread itself and grew without any help from me, that same reluctance arose but Yay! I noticed it and stayed out of the way. It was a joyous time for me, no one else had arrived yet and I was alone with the growing fire feeling like I'd found a really good balance between action and appreciation. And that is like the effort not to think angry thoughts. Sometimes you catch it before it happens, sometimes during, sometimes after.

During our ceremony today, I had a strong impulse to work one-on-one with someone who was having a hard time. I asked myself whence that impulse arose, and what my true motivation was. I could see very clearly that this person was capable of moving past the difficulty, and I wanted to lend a hand with that. And I don't see a problem with that, but today in this circumstance it seemed to me that it was not necessary for me to take that action. If it was that clear to me that the difficulty could be overcome easily, then it would be clear to him too if the desire was there. And if not, it's not my place to push it. It felt to me that I would be in some way building myself up at his expense, rather than giving assistance where it was wanted. So I just stayed out of it, and sure enough he came back and joined us and shared with me afterwards what a wonderful experience that was for him. So it seems to me that it isn't only angry thoughts, it might be helpful thoughts too that actually are not helpful.

## Stand

Yesterday I went down a little farther towards the bottom of the hill where I usually cut wood these days. I drive by here on the way home several times a week and I've had my eye on a stand of trees that survived the big brush fires we had here a couple of years ago. One of them is a real beauty, over 30 feet tall, slender at the base – almost enough wood by itself for one ceremony. So I walked in there – it's probably 200 yards from the road across a little ravine. Difficult walk, bit of a slope, this is going to be hard work. On the way I passed a few other good-looking downed trees and made a note for next week, but I just kept going towards that big tree that had grabbed my attention from the road so many times. Well, I got across the ravine and up to that tree and all around me I could see wood that had been downed by those fires and was still really good and solid, very dry, just perfect.

I left that one standing, let it continue to mark the spot for now anyway, and worked on the wood already on the ground. And as I was cutting it and piling the trunks into a little staging area, getting ready for several hard hikes back up to the road, I thought about the that idea of "standing for" something. This tree stands for – what? As I admire how it still reaches up to the sky even with no leaves, no life you might say, it stands for courage, endurance. In that way the tree itself is a symbol, an indicator of something not directly perceived or physically present. I mean, the tree is probably not actually courageous, at least not in the way we normally use that word. Courage implies some kind of choice to act in the face of danger and fear, doesn't it? This tree stood firm on its foundation right through the midst of a terrible fire. Do I admire the tree? Well not exactly. I do admire what the tree calls forth in my imagination, in my consciousness – I admire what the tree symbolizes for me. I could say this is a buffalo tree, a *tatanka* tree, and that calls forth thoughts and images of the Lakota people over the centuries, standing strong and enduring through massive sometimes cataclysmic changes. I think of those who have taken a stand for their people, who have withstood terrible hardships and remained standing, remained dedicated to the good of their family, their band, village, tribe, country. I think of Martin Luther King, Mahatma Ghandi, Sitting Bull.

As I hefted one of those 10-foot trunk pieces up onto my back and struggled to stand up, once again I felt that wonderful balance and strength that have blessed my weekly efforts so powerfully. When I set out yesterday morning my back and neck were already sore – ironically, I'd been crouching over a computer terminal in a cramped equipment room early in the week for just a bit too long, and it left me with a few pains and some stiffness; carrying these trees up a rocky slope ought to make that worse, you'd think, but actually something about the coordination of the muscles and gravity and whatever was working within me brought relief rather than increased discomfort.

So as I sweated and humped these trees, I thought about what I stand for and as I did, the meanings of that question converged: why am I standing under this heavy load, and what principles do I uphold, and what do I represent? All of these come together somehow in this practice. Sitting Bull said "Oyate kin ya nipi ktaca" – so that the People will *nipi* – "become strong" is the usual translation. The ceremony we do every week is called *inipi* and it does mean to become strong, spiritually, physically, emotionally, mentally. And that is what I try to stand for, that is why I am doing this, what is represented in the choice to perform this ritual each week, starting here with the cutting and gathering of wood as I gather my prayers and prepare for the next day's fire. On the face of it, of course that's why I am doing this – so that the people who come to our lodge will have their ceremony. And also so that the *oyate*, the nation, the community will come forth and become strong. And also so that my family, my *tiyospaye* will come together in that circle and help each other, pray together, be a stand for each other. Inevitably I think of the Sun Dance, which is coming up in less than 2 months, a snap of the fingers. How my life seems to proceed from one Sun Dance to the next – that is what I think of when I think of how my year is going, it's June to June. I long to stand in that circle again with my brothers and sisters – how free we are in the confines of this arduous and strict practice, how joyously we break through the limitations that seem to pervade our lives outside that sacred circle. And it's not, I think, an inflated sense of self to say that we do this for the people; we dance for ourselves, yes, but more so for our families and the greater family of which we are a part – we stand for all the families.

# Extraduction

As you're leaving just let me share one last story with you. This is not a woodcut – it's from much earlier in my life. When I was a senior in high school, I was delighted to accept an invitation to teach 10th-grade math with an introduction to programming and computer science. I had a class full of very bright kids, and one day decided to challenge them with what seems like a simple question in the theory of probability. Here it is:

> *I flip 2 coins and trap them on a table in front of me, one under each hand. You cannot see them. I peek at both of them and tell you that one of them is heads. What is the probability that they are both heads?*

If you're not familiar with probability, for this question all you need to know is this: if you have a bunch of possible outcomes that are equally likely to happen, then the probability of one of them happening is 1 divided by the total number of them. Another way to say that is: if I repeat an action a lot of times, what percentage of the time will that one outcome happen? For example, if I flip one coin, there are 2 equally likely results: heads, and tails. The probability of heads is ½, and so is the probability of tails. So if I flip a coin 1000 times, I'd expect 500 heads and 500 tails. (Yet think about this: if you flip a coin 1000 times and it comes up heads exactly 500 times, wouldn't that seem remarkable, amazing? But I'm getting ahead of myself.)

When you have 2 coins, you take into account every possible combination of the two. There are 4 of them:

| COIN A | COIN B |
|--------|--------|
| H | H |
| T | H |
| H | T |
| T | T |

Of those 4 possibilities, only one of them is "both heads", so if you flip 2 coins, the probability of them both coming up heads is ¼. In the problem I posed to my 10th-graders, one of those possibilities is eliminated – they can't both be tails if one of them is heads. So the answer is 1/3.

Well. You would not believe the controversy stirred up by this little exercise. All I had in mind was to give my students a problem to solve with a computer program – run a whole bunch of trials, throw out any that don't have at least one "heads", and find the percentage that have "both heads". Even after seeing the results, however, several seniors and one or two teachers just *insisted* that the probability of both heads is ¼, and no peeking or telling has anything to do with that. Their position was, you simply ignore any other information, it's not relevant. Meanwhile, the students, their official teacher, some of their parents, and I pointed out that the computer calculation demonstrates very clearly that the probability is 1/3. However – what was and is really interesting to me is not the math, it's the amount of emotional charge that attended the conversation – it was enormous.

Some of the arguments that occurred then, or that occur to me now, include:

Just because someone says one of them is heads doesn't make it true – they could be making that up.

You can't say the probability changes when someone looks at the coins – probability is an objective, calculated quantity, it's not dependent on an observer.

There is no such thing as a calculation of probability that is not dependent on an observer. Probability is not an attribute of an event, it's an attribute of *knowledge*. Based on a calculation of probability, I know what's going to happen in the future, approximately. Not precisely. This is a question of what it means to "know" something.

The future is only the future with respect to the consciousness of the observer. And it's not objective and fixed – if you flip a coin 1000 times, you won't see exactly 500 heads and exactly 500 tails. I mean, you might, but it's no surprise if you don't. Probability is about what might happen *in the future*.

And anyway, "heads" and "tails" are the other way around from the perspective of another observer underneath a glass table looking up.

The probability of a coin coming up heads is ½ - it makes no difference at all what the other coin did.

And so on. Nobody was neutral about this, it really seemed to awaken a deeply held highly-charged *something* in everyone. I think, looking back on it now, that this simple question touches on a fundamental issue for human beings: what is the relationship between what's "out there" and what's "in here"; that is, between existence and consciousness?   If you've looked into quantum mechanics and nuclear physics (and who hasn't?) you know that this question takes on great significance in the search for a fundamental understanding of the nature of matter.

And really that's what these stories have been about, that's the question I've kept coming back to.  What is the relationship between my thoughts, experiences, observations, feelings while cutting the wood and the way of our ceremony the next day?  How is my awareness related to the experiences I have with other people?  To what degree does my intention or attention influence or reflect events in the community where I live? What about the relationship between consciousness and health?  Surely in some way we can all appreciate that these connections are real.

Doesn't it make sense to exercise and nourish my consciousness the way I exercise and nourish my body?  That is the point of a spiritual practice, it seems to me.  It's not about worshipping something or someone "out there", it's about honoring, honing, strengthening the inner guiding spark of life, recognizing it's something that we have in common while at the same time it's unique in each of us – a mystery. A really great mystery.


Aloha!


David